SRI AUROBINDO AND THE MOTHER

ON

LOVE

QUOTATIONS
SELECTED AND PRESENTED
BY PAVITRA

SRI AUROBINDO ASHRAM
PONDICHERRY-INDIA

First edition 1966
Second edition 1973
Revised and Enlarged 1988
Fourth impression 2005

Price: Rs 32
ISBN 81-7058-104-4

© Sri Aurobindo Ashram Trust 1966, 1988
Published by Sri Aurobindo Ashram Publication Department,
Pondicherry - 605 002
Website: http://sabda.sriaurobindoashram.org

Printed at Sri Aurobindo Ashram Press, Pondicherry
PRINTED IN INDIA

If we have a school here, it must be different from the millions of schools in the world; it must give the children a chance to distinguish between ordinary life and divine life, the life of truth—to see things in a different way. It is useless to repeat here the ordinary life. The teachers' mission is to open the eyes of the children to something which they would find nowhere else.

THE MOTHER, *Questions and Answers, Bulletin, November* 1963.

CONTENTS

PREFACE

I DIVINE LOVE AND ITS MANIFESTATION
Page 1

II LOVE IN THE TERRESTRIAL EVOLUTION
Page 14

III PURIFICATION AND LIBERATION OF LOVE
Page 23

IV LOVE AND ANANDA IN THE TRANSFORMED MANIFESTATION
Page 35

GLOSSARY OF SANSKRIT TERMS
Page 47

PREFACE

If there is a problem difficult to solve for the young of both sexes, it is that of love. Sooner or later, as they grow from childhood to adult age, they meet love, feel or observe the vehemence of the crises it raises in the human heart, and try to understand its nature and discover a line of conduct. Adults are hardly wiser; they are as much the plaything of the force that possesses them and seek for a compromise behaviour that would avoid disturbing too much their own existence and society's.

One of the peculiarities of the problem of love for the child is that he (or she) is left almost alone to solve it. He does not find in his class-books any indication about it, and when he turns to a parent, a teacher or an elderly person, the answers that he gets can only puzzle him more. Either he is signed to silence and told not to busy himself with such things: "the less one speaks or thinks of it the better it is." Or he is told that he will understand when "bigger"—which a false promise; grown-ups are not wiser than children, they are only less struck by the newness and strangeness of love's manifestations. As to his talks with class-mates, it is best not to say anything!

At times, rarely, a mother or a father will try to help the child out, but the answers they give are hardly understandable by the child. They raise new questions and the child is drawn along to a strange world, invisible but revealed by its effects in him and around him.

In short, it seems as if everything were conspiring to stifle or repress the silent force, a force that no one can explain or master, but with which one has to come to terms and live.

As the child grows, he realizes that the problem of love is among the greatest concerns of the world. He sees that famous writers have heaped up volumes about it, in praise of its sweetness, or in blame of its violence or simply in describing of its vagaries. His teachers have been obliged to speak of it, but none understands its nature.

Later on, the child may come across a book pretending to throw some light on the problem. He is asked to analyse his dreams and make the Unconscious conscious. A dark sink opens before him; explanations do not satisfy him, they only bring him harassing and disconcerting thoughts.

Finally, the child is led to acknowledge as a fact the existence in him, as in every living being, of a secret force that seems to originate and develop from the animal world. He has to control it, as best he can, and hide away its effects, whatever storms may rage within.

And yet it ought to be relatively easy for us, disciples of Sri Aurobindo and the Mother, to give to such problems as children and adults meet in that domain an explanation which would satisfy them and throw light on what happens within them.

Sri Aurobindo and the Mother have in several places of their works spoken of Love as one of the essential aspects of the Divine and as a fundamental principle of the universe—although still in large part veiled. The fact that Love is only partly revealed hides perhaps from us the role assumed by love in the evolution of the universe and of each individual being of the universe. A small key is required.

The Divine—simultaneously One and Many—manifests himself in the universe through separate centres of consciousness. Without Love these centres would remain eternally separate. Each would evolve in its own way, without deep contact with the others. What would be lacking to it is the consciousness of its identity with the Divine and of its underlying connection with the other centres.

The aspect of the Divine that has taken upon itself the task of bridging this eternal opposition is Love. And love is, in the evolution of the universe, the hidden force that will accomplish the work.

The careful observer—and such is the child—sees manifestations of this force everywhere. He marks its elementary forms in insects and the lower animals. They are then mechanical and reflex: sexual instinct and associative instinct (ants, bees); hunger is also a manifestation of love (one devours what one loves).

Later on, his science books will teach him that attractive forces (and repulsive forces that are complementary) are indispensable to build up matter—the matter of physics and chemistry. Molecules, and even atoms and their constituents, exist only owing to the presence of certain forces that ensure their cohesion. Does not the Mother say that love exists—with consciousness—even in the stone?

In the higher animals—birds, mammals—the mechanical and reflex action is modified by a nascent psychic element (rearing of offspring, faithfulness to a mate, devotion to the pack). Between the higher animal and man, the difference in this sphere is not large; it is in the growth of the mental element (reasoning capacity) that man differs mostly from the animal.

Separation of sexes is but a device used by Nature to reach her own ends. It is not indispensable to the propagation of the species —many species are asexual or bisexual. But this separation is convenient and efficient.

Now each human being—everyone of us—is evolving in the universe through a succession of many lives upon earth, and as the object of this evolution is the progressive awareness of our essential identity with the Divine—One and Many simultaneously—everyone of us will progressively become aware of the essential Love that is in him and of his bonds of love with the other beings.

Then, instead of opposing eternally all others, each of us will feel a natural affinity with this one or that one. All throughout the ages consciousness grows as evolution progresses. One day, the individual being is at last ready to recognize in others the same consciousness that exists in him. He recognizes others as his other selves; he recognizes himself in others and in all. He can at long last understand the meaning of this passage of the Upanishad about the One Self or Spirit everywhere:

"It is not for the sake of the husband that the husband is dear, but for the sake of the *ātman*[1] [which is in him]; it is not for the sake of the wife that the wife is dear but for the sake of the *ātman* [which is in her]...".

Bṛhadāraṇyaka Up.

With the help of these powerful and significant words it is possible to classify individual human beings in one or the other of two groups. Those of the first group—*the outward path*—find in an association with another individual a real help. For them, no problem; they follow instinctively the reactions of Nature in them, and it would be at once unwise and vain to try to change their reactions by advocating a higher path; they would not understand.

Those of the second group—*the return path*—are more advanced in their evolution and feel strongly the attraction of the divine pole in them. For them, a long-standing association with another individual would be contrary to their spiritual destiny and to indulge

---

[1] *The Self, one with the Divine.*

in it would cause delay in the progress of their soul. They cannot commit themselves and alienate their deep-seated freedom.

But the border line between the two groups is not clearly drawn. There is a large category of men and women evolving in a margin of incertitude. These become the seat of a prolonged and painful conflict between the two poles of their being, the human and the divine. But they have to move forward, at whatever cost.

Yoga is a process that accelerates individual evolution. Through yoga those that are treading *the return path*, and even those that are struggling in the zone of incertitude, may clear in one life a great part of the way and reach divine union. The fact of aspiring to yoga is a proof that one is treading *the return path*, or is quite close to it.

With this in mind we understand clearly why Sri Aurobindo and the Mother, speaking to all who follow yoga or aspire to it, repeat constantly that a "vital" or sexual relationship with another individual is one of the greatest obstacles on the way.

This explains also why persons from outside—who do not follow yoga—get an impression when reading the works of Sri Aurobindo and the Mother that they reject human love, vital and sexual, for the whole of mankind. It is now clear that this is a wrong impression. If someone of *the outward path* consults the Mother in order to ascertain whether it is advisable to marry or not, the answer will in general not be negative. And her approval would hold all the more for the innumerable millions of men and women to whom the idea will never come to consult a spiritual leader about their marriage.

These explanations should enable anyone of us, if he observes and studies himself attentively, to ascertain, at least roughly, where he stands on the long scale of evolution. He will not only be able to understand his instinctive reactions, but will also know that, whatever place he has now reached, he will tread the entirety of the scale and attain liberation. Fear drops out of him—that fear of standing forever condemned, contemptible, imperfect. He will be able to look at himself without losing strength and come to decisions accordingly.

This is the light given to us by Sri Aurobindo and the Mother; it is a priceless gift. The following quotations will convince every person of good will.

PAVITRA
(P. B. Saint-Hilaire)

I

DIVINE LOVE AND ITS MANIFESTATION

1.   If Idea embracing Force begot the worlds, Delight of Being begot the Idea. Because the Infinite conceived an innumerable delight in itself, therefore worlds and universes came into existence.
SRI AUROBINDO, Thoughts and Glimpses.

2.   The universe is not merely a mathematical formula for working out the relation of certain mental abstractions called numbers and principles to arrive in the end at a zero or a void unit, neither is it merely a physical operation embodying a certain equation of forces. It is the delight of a Self-lover, the play of a Child, the endless self-multiplication of a Poet intoxicated with the rapture of His own power of endless creation.
Ibid.

3.   There are other great Personalities of the Divine Mother.... There are among them Presences indispensable for the supramental realisation,—most of all one who is her Personality of that mysterious and powerful ecstasy and Ananda which flows from a supreme divine Love, the Ananda that alone can heal the gulf between the highest heights of the supramental spirit and the lowest abysses of Matter, the Ananda that holds the key of a wonderful divinest Life and even now supports from its secrecies the work of all the other Powers of the universe.
SRI AUROBINDO, The Mother, VI.

4.   The manifestation of the love of the Divine in the world was the great holocaust, the supreme self-giving. The

Perfect Consciousness accepted to be merged and absorbed into the unconsciousness of matter, so that consciousness might be awakened in the depths of its obscurity and little by little a Divine Power might rise in it and make the whole of this manifested universe a highest expression of the Divine Consciousness and the Divine Love.

THE MOTHER, *Conversations with the Mother, IX.*

5.   When the Supreme decided to exteriorise himself so that he might see himself, the first thing that he exteriorised out of himself was Knowledge of the world and Power to create it.... In the Supreme Will there was a plan and the first principle of this plan was the expression at once of Delight and Freedom, in their essence, which seemed to be the most interesting character of this creation.... Intermediaries were needed to express this Delight and Freedom through forms. And Four Beings were first brought out to start the world-development which had to be a progressive objectivisation of all that is potentially contained in the Supreme. These Beings[1], in the principle of their being, were Consciousness and Light, Life, Delight and Love, and Truth.... As soon as they began their work, they started having their own conception of the work to be done and how it was to be done. Being wholly free, they chose to do it independently. Instead of taking the attitude of a servant and instrument, they naturally took the attitude of a master, and this lapse, I may say, was the first cause, the essential cause of all disorder in the world. And as soon as there was separation—for that was the essential cause of separation—as soon as there was separation between the Supreme and that which had emanated, Consciousness was changed into unconsciousness, Light into darkness, Love into hate,

---

[1] [They are mentioned in most of the great religious traditions. In the Indian tradition they are known as the ancient or former gods, *pūrve devāḥ*. Sri Aurobindo speaks of them in *On Yoga, II, tome I, pp.* 386 *and* 399. Pavitra]

Delight into suffering, Life into death and Truth into falsehood.... The result is the world as we see it. It has been done progressively, step by step, and it would be really too long to tell you all that; however, the culmination at the end was matter, obscure, inconscient, miserable. The creative Force which had brought out these Four Beings essentially for the creation of the world observed what was happening and turned to the Supreme and implored Him for the remedy and cure of the evil that had been done.

Then the order was given, Consciousness to precipitate into the inconscience, Love into the suffering, Truth into the falsehood. And it was a greater Consciousness, a more total Love, a more perfect Truth than what had emanated in the beginning that now plunged into the horror of matter to awaken there consciousness and love and light, to begin that movement of Redemption which must bring back the material universe to its supreme origin.

THE MOTHER, *Questions and Answers*,
Bulletin, February 1958.

6.   It is with the sense of separation that pain and suffering, misery and ignorance and all the incapacities have come. And it is with self-giving, self-forgetfulness in a total consecration that suffering will disappear and give place to a Delight that nothing can obscure.

It is only when this Delight is established in this world that it can be truly transformed, then only there will be a new life, a new creation, a new realisation. The Delight must first be established in the consciousness, then the material transformation will take place, not before.

Note that I do not speak of what people call delight, which is not even a caricature of true Delight, but rather a diabolical invention to make you lose the way, the delight or joy that comes from pleasure, forgetfulness, indifference. What I speak of is a Delight that is perfect peace, light without shadow, harmony, beauty whole and entire and irresistible power, the

Delight that is the Divine Presence itself, in its essence, in its will and in its realisation.

It is with the Adversary that suffering has come into the world. And it is Delight alone that can conquer it, nothing else can conquer it definitely, finally.

Delight is the creator, Delight is the fulfiller.

THE MOTHER, Questions and Answers,
Bulletin, February 1960.

7.   The world is a masked form of Sachchidananda, and the nature of the consciousness of Sachchidananda, and therefore the thing in which His force must always find and achieve itself is divine Bliss, an omnipresent self-delight.... To seek for delight is therefore the fundamental impulse and sense of Life; to find and possess and fulfil it is its whole motive.... But where in us is this principle of Delight?... That term is something in us which we sometimes call, in a special sense, the soul—that is to say, the psychic entity which is not the life or the mind, much less the body, but which holds in itself the opening and flowering of the essence of all these to their own peculiar delight of self, to light, to love, to joy and beauty and to a refined purity of being.

SRI AUROBINDO, The Life Divine, I,
ch. XXIII.

8.   I do not think that one can say that there was a material substance [before the descent of the divine Love].... The birth of the Inconscient is anterior to the formation of the worlds, and it is only when the perception came that all the universe was going to be created uselessly that there was a call and the divine Love precipitated itself into the Inconscient to change it into Consciousness.... The earthly world, the earth came into existence after the descent into the Inconscient, not before.

THE MOTHER, Questions and Answers,
Bulletin, November 1965.

9. If you are in contact with your psychic being, you begin to feel, to have a kind of perception of what divine Love may be.... Do not try to enter into direct relation with divine Love because it will still be vital desire that pushes you. Perhaps you would not be conscious of it, but it would be a vital desire. You must make an effort to come in contact with your psychic being in order to be conscious and free in the consciousness of your psychic being, and then quite naturally, spontaneously you will know what divine Love is.

Ibid.

10. The phrase "central being" in our yoga is usually applied to the portion of the Divine in us which supports all the rest and survives through death and birth. This central being has two forms—above, it is the Jivatman, our true being, of which we become aware when the higher knowledge comes, —below, it is the psychic being which stands behind mind, body and life. The Jivatman is above the manifestation in life and presides over it; the psychic being stands behind the manifestation in life and supports it.

The natural attitude of the psychic being is to feel itself as the Child, the Son of God, the Bhakta; it is a portion of the Divine, one in essence, but in the dynamics of the manifestation there is always even in identity a difference. The Jivatman, on the contrary, lives in the essence and can merge itself in identity with the Divine; but it too, the moment it presides over the dynamics of the manifestation, knows itself as one centre of the multiple Divine, not as the Parameshwara.

SRI AUROBINDO, *On Yoga, II, tome I, part I, 5.*

(It is because the Divine has descended into the material world and infused the redeeming principle into it that the earth has become a world where evolution is the natural law; the psychic being is thus the sign and result of the great holocaust. P)

11. There is and can be no psychic being in a non-evolutionary creature like the Asura; there can be none in a god who does not need one for his existence.... If any being of the typal worlds wants to evolve, he has to come down to earth and take a human body and accept to share in the evolution. It is because they do not want to do this that the vital beings try to possess men in order that they may enjoy the materialities of physical life without having the burden of the evolution or the process of conversion in which it culminates.
SRI AUROBINDO, On Yoga, II, tome I, part I, 6.

12. The divine Love is there, with all its intensity, all its power, a formidable power, but who is aware of it?... You are literally bathing in an atmosphere altogether vibrant with divine Love and you are not aware of it!... Your vision of the universe is that you are at the centre and the universe all round. It is not the universe that you see, it is you whom you see in the universe. Then, as you are full of yourself, there is no room for the Divine.... But he is there always.
THE MOTHER, Questions and Answers, II,
Bulletin, November 1959.

13. Love is not sexual intercourse.
Love is not vital attraction and interchange.
Love is not the heart's hunger for affection.
Love is a mighty vibration coming straight from the One, and only the very pure and very strong are capable of receiving and manifesting it.

To be pure is to be open only to the Supreme's influence and to no other.
THE MOTHER, Bulletin, Nov. 1963, p. 25.

14. Love is in its nature the desire to give oneself to others and to receive others in exchange.... Physical life does not desire to give itself, it desires only to receive.... Love at first obeys the law of hunger and enjoys the receiving and the exacting from others rather than the giving and surrendering to others which it admits chiefly as a necessary price for the thing that it desires.... Its true law is to establish an equal commerce in which the joy of giving is equal to the joy of receiving and tends in the end to become even greater; but that is when it is shooting beyond itself under the pressure of the psychic flame to attain to the fulfilment of utter unity and has therefore to realise that which seemed to it not-self as an even greater and dearer self than its own individuality.

SRI AUROBINDO, *The Life Divine, I, ch. XXI.*

15. Love is one of the great universal forces; it exists by itself and its movement is free and independent of the objects in which and through which it manifests.... Men think that they have suddenly fallen in love; they see their love come and grow and then it fades—or, it may be, endures a little longer in some who are more specially fitted for its more lasting movement.... Love does not manifest in human beings alone; it is everywhere. Its movement is there in plants, perhaps in the very stones; in the animals it is easy to detect its presence.... Love divine gives itself and asks for nothing. What human beings have made of it, we do not need to say; they have turned it into an ugly and repulsive thing. And yet in human beings the first contact of love does bring down something of its purer substance; they become capable for a moment of forgetting themselves, for a moment its divine touch awakens and magnifies all that is fine and beautiful. But afterwards there comes to the surface the human nature, full of its impure demands, asking for something in exchange, bartering what it gives, clamouring for its own inferior satisfactions, distorting and soiling what was divine.

Conversations with the Mother, IX.

16. There is concealed behind individual love, obscured by its ignorant human figure, a mystery which the mind cannot

seize, the mystery of the body of the Divine, the secret of a mystic form of the Infinite which we can approach only through the ecstasy of the heart and the passion of the pure and sublimated sense, and its attraction which is the call of the divine Flute-player, the mastering compulsion of the All-Beautiful can only be seized and seize us through an occult love and yearning which in the end makes one the Form and the Formless, and identifies Spirit and Matter. It is that which the spirit in Love is seeking here in the darkness of the Ignorance and it is that which it finds when individual human love is changed into the love of the Immanent Divine incarnate in the material universe.

Sri Aurobindo, *The Synthesis of Yoga, I, ch. VI.*

[Commenting on the above passage in the *Bulletin, February* 1961, *Questions and Answers,* the Mother says:]

17.   Krishna the divine Flute-player is the immanent and universal Divine who is the supreme power of attraction; and Radha the soul, the psychic personality answers to the call of the Flute-player.... But as soon as there is the perfect identification all that vanishes... the story comes to its end and there is nothing more to relate. That is why it has been said that if the world, if the creation realised perfect identity with the Divine, there would be no more creation.... The solution [of this contradiction] is to find the Ananda in the very midst of the Play where one gives and takes, where one seems to be two; this is why the Vaishnavas and the mystics keep the taste of the duality. Otherwise in identity there is only identity. If the identity is complete and perfect there is no more objectivisation.

I have already said... that *that* begins by the Ananda of identity and at the end of the entire circuit of creation *that* ends in the Ananda of the union. Had there been no circuit, there would never have been the Ananda of the union; there would only have been the Ananda of identity.

18. KRISHNA

At last I find a meaning of soul's birth
    Into this universe terrible and sweet,
I who have felt the hungry heart of earth
    Aspiring beyond heaven to Krishna's feet.

I have seen the beauty of immortal eyes,
    And heard the passion of the Lover's flute,
And known a deathless ecstasy's surprise
    And sorrow in my heart for ever mute.

Nearer and nearer now the music draws,
    Life shudders with a strange felicity;
All Nature is a wide enamoured pause
    Hoping her lord to touch, to clasp, to be.

For this one moment lived the ages past;
The world now throbs fulfilled in me at last.
Sri Aurobindo, Last Poems.

19. [It is] a very old tradition, older than the two known lines of tradition from the spiritual and occult point of view, that is to say the Vedic and the Chaldean lines, a tradition which seems to have been at the origin of these two known traditions and in which it is said that when the world, because of the action of the adverse forces—the Asuras of Indian tradition—was plunged into the obscurity, inconscience and ignorance that we know, instead of developing in the natural law of Light and Consciousness, the creative Power implored the supreme Origin asking for a special intervention that would be able to save this corrupt universe. And in answer to this prayer, a special Entity emanated from the supreme Origin, an Entity made of Love and Consciousness that was projected directly into the most inconscient matter to begin the work of reawakening to the original Consciousness and Love.

In ancient narratives, this Being is described as lying stretched in deep sleep at the bottom of a dark cave and from it as it lay asleep emanated rays of prismatic light which spread gradually into the Inconscience and was lodged in every element of the Inconscience so that it may start its work of Reawakening.

If you consciously enter this Inconscient, you can still see the same marvellous Being, ever lying in deep sleep and continuing its work of emanation, spreading its light; it will continue to do it until Inconscience is no longer Inconscience, until Obscurity disappears from the world and all creation awakes to the Supramental Consciousness.

And it is worth noticing that this marvellous Being strangely resembles the person whom I saw in vision one day, the Being who is at the other extremity, at the limit of the form and the formless. But this one was in his golden crimson glory whereas the other one in his sleep was diamond white emanating opal rays.

It is this one who is the origin of all Avatars. He is, so to say, the original and universal Avatar who has gradually put on bodies more and more conscious and in the end has manifested in the somewhat known line of Beings who descended directly from the Supreme to perfect the work of preparing the world so that it might, by continuous progress, be ready to receive and manifest the Supramental Light in its entirety.

In every country, in every tradition this fact has been presented in a particular way with different restrictions, different details, individual specialities, but in reality the origin of all the stories is the same, and that is what we may call a direct and conscious intervention of the Supreme in the obscurest matter without passing through intermediaries to awaken this matter to aspiration towards divine Forces.

The interval separating these different incarnations seems to become shorter and shorter, as if matter being more and more ready, the action could hasten and its movement become quicker and quicker, also more and more conscious, more and more effective and decisive.

And this action will go on multiplying and intensifying itself until the whole world becomes the full Avatar of the Supreme.
THE MOTHER, *Questions and Answers,*
Bulletin, August 1958.

20.   Avatarhood would have little meaning if it were not connected with the evolution. The Hindu procession of the ten Avatars is itself, as it were, a parable of evolution. First the Fish Avatar, then the amphibian animal between land and water, then the land animal, then the Man-Lion Avatar, bridging man and animal, then man as a dwarf, small and undeveloped and physical but containing in himself the godhead and taking possession of existence, then the rajasic, sattwic, nirguna Avatars, leading the human development from the vital rajasic to the sattwic mental man and again to the overmental superman. Krishna, Buddha and Kalki depict the last three stages, the stages of the spiritual development—Krishna opens the possibility of overmind, Buddha tries to shoot beyond to the supreme liberation but that liberation is still negative, not returning upon earth to complete positively the evolution; Kalki is to correct this by bringing the Kingdom of the Divine upon earth, destroying the opposing Asura forces. The progression is striking and unmistakable.

As for the lives in between the Avatar lives, it must be remembered that Krishna speaks of many lives in the past, not only a few supreme ones, and secondly while he speaks of himself as the Divine, in one passage he describes himself as a Vibhuti.... We may therefore fairly assume that in many lives he manifested as a Vibhuti veiling the fuller Divine Consciousness. If we admit that the object of Avatarhood is to lead the evolution, this is quite reasonable, the Divine appearing as Avatar in the great transitional stages and as Vibhutis to aid the lesser transition.

SRI AUROBINDO, *On Yoga, II, tome I,*
part I, 7.

21. The Avatar comes as the manifestation of the divine nature in the human nature, the apocalypse of its Christhood, Krishnahood, Buddhahood, in order that the human nature may by moulding its principle, thought, feeling, action, being on the lines of that Christhood, Krishnahood, Buddhahood transfigure itself into the divine. The law, the Dharma which the Avatar establishes is given for that purpose chiefly; the Christ, Krishna, Buddha stands in its centre as the gate, he makes through himself the way men shall follow. That is why each Incarnation holds before men his own example and declares of himself that he is the way and the gate; he declares too the oneness of his humanity with the divine being, declares that the Son of Man and the Father above from whom he has descended are one, that Krishna in the human body and the supreme Lord and friend of all creatures are but two revelations of the same divine Purushottama, revealed there in his own being, revealed here in the type of humanity.

SRI AUROBINDO, *Essays on the Gita, I,* 15.

22. [It is an ancient Chaldean legend.] A very long time ago, in the barren country that is now Arabia, a divine Being became incarnate to awaken the earth to the supreme Love. Of course, he was persecuted by men, harried, suspected, misunderstood. Mortally wounded by his assailants, he wanted to die alone and quietly so that he might complete his task. Being pursued, he ran; all of a sudden in the vast bare plain, he came across a small pomegranate bush. The Saviour crept in among the lower branches, so that he might leave his body in peace; and all at once the bush grew miraculously, became broad, thick and deep, and when the pursuers arrived there, they did not suspect that the man they were hunting for was hiding in it and they went along.

As the sacred blood fell drop by drop, fertilizing the earth, the tree blossomed out with marvellous, large flowers, covering the ground with their petals, innumerable drops of blood.

These are the flowers that for us express and contain the divine Love.

     THE MOTHER, *Message of* 14th *November* 1955.

23. Men's way of doing things well is through a clear mental connection; they see things and do things with the mind and what they want is a mental and human perfection. When they think of a manifestation of Divinity, they think it must be an extraordinary perfection in doing ordinary human things—an extraordinary business faculty, political, poetic or artistic faculty, an accurate memory, not making mistakes, not undergoing any defect or failure. Or else they think of things which they call superhuman like not eating food or telling cotton-futures or sleeping on nails or eating them [one could add many other things, such as curing diseases or making pass an examination successfully. Pavitra.] All that has nothing to do with manifesting the Divine.... These human ideas are false.

The Divinity acts according to another consciousness, the consciousness of the Truth above and the Lila below and It acts according to the need of the Lila, not according to man's ideas of what It should or should not do. This is the first thing one must grasp, otherwise one can understand nothing about the manifestation of the Divine.

     SRI AUROBINDO, *On Yoga, II, tome I,*
           part II, 7.

II

LOVE IN THE TERRESTRIAL EVOLUTION

24. THE MIRACLE OF BIRTH

I saw my soul a traveller through Time;
    From life to life the cosmic way it trod,
Obscure in the depths and on the heights sublime,
    Evolving from the worm into the god.

A spark of the eternal Fire, it came
    To build a house in Matter for the Unborn.
The inconscient sunless Night received the flame,
    In the brute seed of things dumb and forlorn

Life stirred and Thought outlined a gleaming shape
    Till on the stark inanimate earth could move,
Born to somnambulist Nature in her sleep,
    A thinking creature who can hope and love.

Still by slow steps the miracle goes on,
The Immortal's gradual birth mid mire and stone.
                SRI AUROBINDO, *Last Poems.*

25.   At the beginning of this manifestation, Love is, in the purity of its origin, composed of two movements, two complementary poles of the impulsion towards complete fusion. On one side, it is the supreme power of attraction and on the other the irresistible need of absolute self-giving.... What was projected into space had to be brought back to itself without, however, destroying the universe so created. Therefore Love burst forth, the irresistible power of union....

Is it not love, under an erring and obscure form, that is associated with all the impulsions of the physical and vital nature as the push towards every movement and every grouping? This has become quite visible in the plant world. In the plant and the tree, it is the need of growth to get more light, more air, more space; in the flower it is the gift of beauty and fragrance in a loving efflorescence. And in the animal is it not there behind hunger and thirst, the need for appropriation, expansion, procreation, in brief behind all desire, whether conscious or not? And, among the higher orders, in the self-sacrificing devotion of the female for her young ones? This naturally leads us to the human species where, with the triumphant advent of mental activity this association attains its climax, for it is there conscious and deliberate....

It is also from this very moment that there has clearly appeared in Nature's works her will to build up again, by stages and degrees, the primordial unity through groupings more and more complex and numerous. She used the power of love for bringing two human beings together and creating the dual group, the origin of family. Once she had broken the narrow limits of personal egoism by changing it into a dual egoism, she brought into being, with the appearance of the child, a more complex unit, the family. In course of time through manifold association between families, interchange between individuals and blood mixture, larger groupings appeared: the clan, the tribe, the caste and the class to end in the creation of the nation. The work of group formation proceeded simultaneously in different parts of the world; it has crystallised in the formation of different races. Even these races Nature will by degrees fuse together in her endeavour to build a material and real basis for human unity.

THE MOTHER, *The Four Austerities and the Four Liberations, III.*

26. Man seeks at first blindly and does not even know that he is seeking his divine Self; for he starts from the obscurity of material Nature and even when he begins to see, he is long

blinded by the light that is increasing in him. God too answers obscurely to his search; He seeks and enjoys man's blindness like the hands of a little child that grope after its mother.

SRI AUROBINDO, *Thoughts and Glimpses*.

27. Man is in love with pleasure; therefore he must undergo the yoke of grief and pain. For unmixed delight is only for the free and passionless soul; but that which pursues after pleasure in man is a suffering and straining energy.

Ibid.

28. Death is the question Nature puts continually to Life and her reminder to it that it has not yet found itself. If there were no siege of death, the creature would be bound for ever in the form of an imperfect living. Pursued by death he awakes to the idea of perfect life and seeks out its means and its possibility.

Ibid.

29. Pain is the touch of our Mother teaching us how to bear and grow in rapture. She has three stages of her schooling, endurance first, next equality of soul, last ecstasy.

SRI AUROBINDO, *Thoughts and Aphorisms*, 93.

30. Pain and grief are Nature's reminder to the soul that the pleasure it enjoys is only a feeble hint of the real delight of existence. In each pain and torture of our being is the secret of a flame of rapture compared with which our greatest pleasures are only as dim flickerings. It is this secret which forms the attraction for the soul of great ordeals, sufferings and fierce experiences of life which the nervous mind in us shuns and abhors.

SRI AUROBINDO, *Thoughts and Glimpses*.

31.   When I see others suffer, I feel that I am unfortunate, but the wisdom that is not mine, sees the good that is coming and approves.

> SRI AUROBINDO, *Thoughts and Aphorisms*, 25.

32.   Hatred is the sign of a secret attraction that is eager to flee from itself and furious to deny its own existence. That too is God's play in His creature.

> SRI AUROBINDO, *Thoughts and Aphorisms*, 113.

33.   What is usually called love is as far from the central vibration of true love as hatred; only one contracts, stiffens, the other strikes out, that is all the difference.

> THE MOTHER, *A Propos, Bulletin, February* 1966.

34.   This world was built by cruelty that she might love. Wilt thou abolish cruelty? Then love too will perish, but thou mayst transfigure it into its opposite, into a fierce love and delightfulness.

> SRI AUROBINDO, *Thoughts and Aphorisms*, 89.

35. LIFE UNITY

I housed within my heart the life of things,
    All hearts athrob in the world I felt as mine;
I shared the joy that in creation sings
    And drank its sorrow like a poignant wine.

I have felt the anger in another's breast,
    All passions poured through my world-self their waves;
One love I shared in a million bosoms expressed.
    I am the beast man slays, the beast he saves.

> I spread life's burning wings of rapture and pain;
>> Black fire and gold fire strove towards one bliss:
> I rose by them towards a supernal plane
>> Of power and love and deathless ecstasies.
>
> A deep spiritual calm no touch can sway
> Upholds the mystery of this Passion-play.
>> SRI AUROBINDO, *Last Poems*.

36. God has opened my eyes; for I saw the nobility of the vulgar, the attractiveness of the repellent, the perfection of the maimed and the beauty of the hideous.
> SRI AUROBINDO, *Thoughts and Aphorisms*, 20.

37. To feel and love the God of beauty and good in the ugly and the evil, and still yearn in utter love to heal it of its ugliness and its evil, this is real virtue and morality.
> SRI AUROBINDO, *Thoughts and Aphorisms*, 49.

38. To hate the sinner is the worst sin, for it is hating God; yet he who commits it glories in his superior virtue.
> SRI AUROBINDO, *Thoughts and Aphorisms*, 50.

39. I have forgotten what vice is and what virtue; I can only see God, His play in the world and His will in humanity.
> SRI AUROBINDO, *Thoughts and Aphorisms*, 29.

40. Sin is that which was once in its place, persisting now it is out of place; there is no other sinfulness.
> SRI AUROBINDO, *Thoughts and Aphorisms*, 66.

41. Humanity has the sexual impulse; that is altogether natural, spontaneous, and, if I may say, legitimate. This impulse will naturally and spontaneously disappear with animality [in man].... The most conscious impulse in a superior humanity, that which has persisted as a source of—bliss is too big a word—joy, delight, is certainly the sexual activity. It will have absolutely no reason for existence in the functions of nature, when the need to create in that way will no longer exist.... But what the ancient spiritual aspirants had sought on principle—sexual negation—is an absurd thing, because this must be only for those who have gone beyond that stage and have no longer animality in them. And it must drop naturally without effort and without struggle. It is only when the consciousness ceases to be human that it drops off naturally. Here also there is a transition that may be somewhat difficult, because beings of transition are always in an unstable equilibrium; but within there is a kind of flame and a need which makes it not painful—it is not painful effort, it is something that one can do with a smile. But to seek to impose it upon those who are not ready for this transition is absurd.

THE MOTHER, *Notes on the Way,*
Bulletin, Feb. 1966.

42. TO X FOR HER MARRIAGE

To unite your physical existences and your material interests, to associate yourselves so as to face together the difficulties and successes, the defeats and victories of life—this is the very basis of marriage—but you know already that it does not suffice.

To be united in feelings, to have the same tastes and same aesthetic pleasures, to vibrate together in a common response to the same things, one by the other and one for the other—it is good, it is necessary—but it is not enough.

To be one in profound sentiments, your affections, your feelings of tenderness for each other not varying in spite of all the shocks of existence; withstanding weariness, nervous irritations and disappointments, to be always and in every case happy, most happy to be together; to find, under all circumstances, one in the presence of the other, rest peace and joy—it is good, it is very good, it is indispensable—but it is not enough.

To unite your mentalities, your thoughts harmonising and becoming complementary to each other, your intellectual preoccupations and discoveries shared between you; in a word, to make your spheres of mental activity identical through a broadening and an enrichment acquired by the two at the same time—it is good, it is absolutely necessary—but it is not enough.

Beyond it all, at the bottom, at the centre, at the summit of the being, there is a Supreme Truth of the being, an Eternal Light, independent of all circumstances of birth, of country, of environment, of education; the origin, cause and master of our spiritual development—it is That that gives a definite orientation to our existence; it is That that decides our destiny; it is in the consciousness of this that you should unite. To be one in aspiration and ascension, to advance with the same step on the spiritual path—such is the secret of a durable union.

THE MOTHER in *Mother India, Oct.* 1966.

43.   Sex is a movement of general Nature seeking for its play and it uses this or that one—a man vitally or physically "in love" as it is called with a woman is simply repeating and satisfying the world-movement of sex; if it had not been that woman, it would have been another.

SRI AUROBINDO, *On Yoga, II, tome II,* 7.

44.   The terrestrial sex-movement is a utilisation by Nature of the fundamental physical energy for the purposes of procreation. The thrill of which the poets speak, which is accompanied by a very gross excitement, is the lure by which she makes the vital consent to this otherwise unpleasing process; there are numbers who experience a recoil of disgust after the act and repulsion from the partner in it because of the disgust, though they return to it when the disgust has worn off for the

sake of this lure.

The sex energy itself is a great power with two components in its physical basis, one meant for procreation and the process necessary for it, the other for feeding the general energies of the body, mind and vital—also the spiritual energies of the body. The old yogis call these two components *retas* and *ojas*.
Ibid.

45. It is the ordinary nature of vital love not to last or, if it tries to last, not to satisfy, because it is a passion which Nature has thrown in in order to serve a temporary purpose; it is good enough therefore for a temporary purpose and its normal tendency is to wane when it has sufficiently served Nature's purpose. In mankind, as man is a more complex being, she calls in the aid of imagination and idealism to help her push, gives a sense of ardour, of beauty and fire and glory, but all that wanes after a time. It cannot last, because it is all a borrowed light and power, borrowed in the sense of being a reflection caught from something beyond and not native to the reflecting vital medium which imagination uses for the purpose. Moreover, nothing lasts in the mind and vital, all is a flux there. The one thing that endures is the soul, the spirit. Therefore love can last and satisfy only if it bases itself on the soul and spirit, if it has its roots there. But that means living no longer in the vital, but in the soul and spirit.
SRI AUROBINDO, *On Yoga, II, tome I, part II*, 7.

46. Human love is mostly vital and physical with a mental support—it can take an unselfish, noble and pure form and expression only if it is touched by the psychic. It is true, as you say, that it is more usually a mixture of ignorance, attachment, passion and desire... there is such a thing as psychic love, pure, without demand, sincere in self-giving, but it is not usually left pure in the attraction of human beings to one another.
Ibid.

47. It is certainly easier to have friendship between man and man or between woman and woman than between man and woman, because there the sexual intrusion is normally absent. In a friendship between man and woman the sexual turn can at any moment come in a subtle or in a direct way and produce perturbations. But there is no impossibility of friendship between man and woman pure of this element; such friendships can exist and have always existed. All that is needed is that the lower vital should not look in at the back door or be permitted to enter.

Ibid.

III

PURIFICATION AND LIBERATION OF LOVE

48. COSMIC CONSCIOUSNESS

I have wrapped the wide world in my wider self
    And Time and Space my spirit's seeing are.
I am the god and demon, ghost and elf,
    I am the wind's speed and the blazing star.
All Nature is the nursling of my care,
    I am its struggle and the eternal rest;
The world's joy thrilling runs through me, I bear
    The sorrow of millions in my lonely breast.
I have learned a close identity with all,
    Yet am by nothing bound that I become;
Carrying in me the universe's call
    I mount to my imperishable home.
I pass beyond Time and life on measureless wings,
Yet still am one with born and unborn things.
                  SRI AUROBINDO, *Last Poems*.

49. When we have passed beyond enjoyings, then we shall have Bliss. Desire was the helper; Desire is the bar.
                  SRI AUROBINDO, *Thoughts and Glimpses*.

50. Transform enjoying into an even and objectless ecstasy; let all thyself be bliss. This is thy goal.
                  Ibid.

51. Love (at least the thing to which human beings give that name) is especially looked upon as an imperious master whose caprices one cannot evade, who strikes you as he pleases and compels you to obey him whether you like it or not. In the name of love the worst crimes have been perpetrated, the wildest follies committed.

And yet, man has invented all kinds of moral and social rules hoping to control this force of love, to make it sober and docile. These rules, however, seem to have been made only to be broken and the restraint they impose upon its free activity seems only to increase its explosive power. For it is not by rules that the movements of love can be governed. Only a greater, higher and truer power of love can master the uncontrollable impulses of love. Love alone can rule over love by illumining, transforming and enlarging it. For here also, more than anywhere else, control consists not in suppressing and abolishing, but in transmuting through a sublime alchemy. This is because, of all forces acting in the universe, love is the most powerful, the most irresistible; without love the world would fall back into the chaos of inconscience. Consciousness is indeed the creator of the universe, but love is its saviour.

THE MOTHER, The Four Austerities
and the Four Liberations, III.

52.   The aim here is fulfilment of the Divine in life and for that, union and solidarity are indispensable. The ideal of the yoga is that all should be centred in and around the Divine and the life of the sadhaks must be founded on that firm foundation, their personal relations also should have the Divine for their centre.... Whatever relations they have with each other, all jealousy, strife, hatred, aversion, rancour and other evil vital feelings should be abandoned.... So, also, all egoistic love and attachment will have to disappear—the love that loves only for the ego's sake and, as soon as the ego is hurt and dissatisfied, ceases to love or even cherishes rancour and hate....

It is not that one cannot have relations with people outside the circle of the sadhaks, but there too if the spiritual life grows within, it must necessarily affect the relation and spiritualise it on the sadhak's side. And there must be no such attachment as would make the relation an obstacle or a rival to the Divine.

Attachment to family often is like that and, if so, it falls away from the sadhak. That is an exigence which, I think, should not be considered excessive. All that, however, can be progressively done; a severing of existing relations is necessary for some, it is not so for all. A transformation, however gradual, is indispensable, severance where severance is the right thing to do.

SRI AUROBINDO, On Yoga, II, tome I,
part II, 8.

53. No error can be more perilous than to accept the immixture of the sexual desire and some kind of subtle satisfaction of it and look on this as a part of the sadhana. It would be the most effective way to head straight towards spiritual downfall and throw into the atmosphere forces that would block the supramental descent, bringing instead the descent of adverse vital powers to disseminate disturbance and disaster....

It is an error too to imagine that, although the physical sexual action is to be abandoned, yet some inward reproduction of it is part of the transformation of the sex-centre. The action of the animal sex-energy in Nature is a device for a particular purpose in the economy of the material creation in the Ignorance. But the vital excitement that accompanies it makes the most favourable opportunity and vibration in the atmosphere for the inrush of those very vital forces and beings whose whole business is to prevent the descent of the supramental Light. The pleasure attached to it is a degradation and not a true form of divine Ananda. The true divine Ananda in the physical has a different quality and movement and substance; self-existent in its essence, its manifestation is dependent only on an inner union with the Divine.... Divine Love, when it touches the physical, does not awaken the gross lower vital propensities; indulgence of them would only repel it and make it withdraw again to the heights from which it is already difficult enough to draw it down into the coarseness of the material creation which it alone can transform.... Seek the divine Love through the only gate through which it will consent to enter, the gate of the psychic being, and cast away the lower vital error.

"Sri Aurobindo Says", *Bulletin*,
August 1965.

54. The Mother has already told you the truth about this idea. The idea that by fully indulging the sex hunger it will be finished and disappear for ever is a deceptive pretence held out by the vital to the mind in order to get a sanction for its desire; it has no other *raison d'être* or truth or justification. If an occasional indulgence keeps the sex desire simmering, a full indulgence would only sink you in its mire. This hunger like other hungers does not cease by temporary satiation; it revives itself after a temporary abeyance and wants again indulgence. Neither sops nor gorgings are the right treatment for it. It can only go by a radical psychic rejection or a full spiritual opening with the increasing descent of a consciousness that does not want it and has a truer Ananda.

SRI AUROBINDO, *Life-Literature-Yoga*,
2nd Ed., *p*. 27.

55. As to sexual impulse, regard it not as something horrible and attractive at the same time, but as a mistake and wrong movement of the lower nature.

SRI AUROBINDO, *On Yoga, II, tome II,* 7.

56. As to the sexual impulse, for this also you must have no moral horror or puritanic or ascetic repulsion. This also is a power of life and while you have to throw away the present form of this power (that is the physical act), the force itself has to be mastered and transformed. It is often strongest in people with a strong vital nature and this strong vital nature can be made a great instrument for the physical realisation of the Divine Life. If the sexual impulse comes, do not be sorry or troubled but look at it calmly, quiet it down, reject all wrong suggestions connected with it and wait for the Higher Con-

sciousness to transform it into the free force and Ananda.
An unpublished letter of SRI AUROBINDO,
in *Mother India, Oct.* 1967.

57.   If she consents to marry, that would be the best. All these vital disturbances proceed from suppressed sex-instinct, suppressed but not rejected and overcome.

A mental acceptance or enthusiasm for the sadhana is not a sufficient guarantee nor sufficient ground for calling people, especially young people, to begin it. Afterwards these vital instincts rise up and there is nothing sufficient to balance or prevail against them,—only mental ideas which do not prevail against the instincts, but on the other hand, also stand in the way of the natural social means of satisfaction. If she marries now and gets experience of the human vital life, then thereafter there may be a chance of her mental aspiration for sadhana turning into the real thing.
"*Sri Aurobindo Says*", in *Bulletin,
November* 1967.

58.   Absence of love and fellow-feeling is not necessary for nearness to the Divine; on the contrary, a sense of closeness and oneness with others is a part of the divine consciousness into which the sadhak enters by nearness to the Divine and the feeling of oneness with the Divine.... In this yoga the feeling of unity with others, love, universal joy and Ananda are an essential part of the liberation and perfection which are the aim of the sadhana.
SRI AUROBINDO, *On Yoga, II, tome I,
part II,* 8.

59.   This is a miracle that men can love God, yet fail to love humanity. With whom are they in love then?
SRI AUROBINDO, *Thoughts and
Aphorisms,* 52.

60. The love which is turned towards the Divine ought not to be the usual vital feeling which men call by that name; for that is not love, but only a vital desire, an instinct of appropriation, the impulse to possess and monopolise. Not only is this not the divine Love, but it ought not to be allowed to mix in the least degree in the yoga. The true love for the Divine is a self-giving, free of demand, full of submission and surrender; it makes no claim, imposes no condition, strikes no bargain, indulges in no violences of jealousy or pride or anger—for these things are not in its composition. In return the Divine Mother also gives herself, but freely... her presence in your mind, your vital, your physical consciousness, her power re-creating you in the divine nature, taking up all the movements of your being and directing them towards perfection and fulfilment, her love enveloping you and carrying you in its arms Godwards. It is this that you must aspire to feel and possess in all your parts down to the very material, and here there is no limitation either of time or of completeness. If one truly aspires and gets it there ought to be no room for any other claim or for any disappointed desire.

SRI AUROBINDO, *On Yoga, II, tome I, part II*, 7.

61. The Mother did not tell you that love is not an emotion, but that Divine Love is not an emotion,—a very different thing to say. Human love is made up of emotion, passion and desire,—all of them vital movements, therefore bound to the disabilities of the human vital nature. Emotion is an excellent and indispensable thing in human nature, in spite of all its shortcomings and dangers.... But our aim is to go beyond emotion to the height and depth and intensity of the Divine Love and there feel through the inner psychic heart an inexhaustible oneness with the Divine which the spasmodic leapings of the vital emotion cannot reach or experience.

SRI AUROBINDO, *On Yoga, II, tome I, part II*, 7.

62.   It is... a mistake to think that the vital alone has warmth and the psychic is something frigid without any flame in it. A clear limpid goodwill is a very good and desirable thing. But that is not what is meant by psychic love. Love is love and not merely goodwill. Psychic love can have a warmth and a flame as intense and more intense than the vital, only it is a pure fire, not dependent on the satisfaction of ego-desire or on the eating up of the fuel it embraces. It is a white flame, not a red one; but white heat is not inferior to the red variety in its ardour. It is true that the psychic love does not usually get its full play in human relations and human nature; it finds the fullness of its fire and ecstasy more easily when it is lifted towards the Divine.

Ibid.

63. THE RUNGS OF LOVE

At first one loves only when one is loved.

Next, one loves spontaneously but one wants to be loved in return.

Further on, one loves even if one is not loved but one still wants one's love to be accepted.

And finally one loves purely and simply without any other need or joy than that of loving.

THE MOTHER, *Bulletin, April* 1966.

64.   You feel lonely because you want to be loved. Learn the joy of loving without demand, just for the *joy of loving* (the most wonderful joy in the world!) and you will never more feel lonely.

Ibid.

65.   When the vital joins in the love for the Divine, it brings into it heroism, enthusiasm, intensity, absoluteness, exclusiveness, the spirit of self-sacrifice, the total and passionate

self-giving of all the nature. It is the vital passion for the Divine that creates the spiritual heroes, conquerors or martyrs.
Sri Aurobindo, *On Yoga, II, tome I, part II,* 8.

66. All renunciation is for a greater joy yet ungrasped. Some renounce for the joy of duty done, some for the joy of peace, some for the joy of God and some for the joy of self-torture, but renounce rather as a passage to the freedom and untroubled rapture beyond.
Sri Aurobindo, *Thoughts and Aphorisms,* 94.

67. In each pain and torture of our being is the secret of a flame of rapture compared with which our greatest pleasures are only as dim flickerings.
Sri Aurobindo, *Thoughts and Glimpses.*

68. So long as the whole consciousness is not clear of doubtful stuff and the realisation of oneness confirmed in the supreme purity, the expression of the all-love is not advisable. It is by holding it in oneself that it becomes a real part of the nature, established and purified by joining with it the other realisations still to come. What you feel is only a first touch and to dissipate it by expression would be very imprudent. The sex and the vital might easily become active—I have known cases of very good yogis... in whom the *viśvaprema* became the *viśvakāma*, all-love becoming all-lust. This has happened with many both in Europe and the East. Even apart from that it is always best to solidify and confirm rather than to throw out and disperse. When the sadhana has progressed and the Knowledge from above comes to enlighten and guide the love, then it will be another matter. My insistence on rejection of all untransformed vital movements is based on experience, mine and others' and that of past yogas like the Vaishnava movement of Chaitanya (not to speak of the old Buddhist

Sahaja dharma) which ended in much corruption. A wide movement such as that of all-love can only take place when the ground of Nature has been solidly prepared for it. I have no objection to your mixing with others, but only under a continual guard and control by a vigilant mind and will.

SRI AUROBINDO, On Yoga, II, tome I, part II, 8.

69. We should not hesitate to open ourselves... to whatever experience of the Infinite we have, to purify and intensify it, to make it our object of constant thought and contemplation, till it becomes the originating power that acts in us, the Godhead we adore and embrace, our whole being is put into tune with it and it is made the very self of our being.... It will turn all that is into itself, reveal itself as the universal Ananda Brahman and make all existence its outpouring. If we wait upon it for the inspiration of all our inner and outer acts, it will become the joy of the Divine pouring itself through us in light and love and power on life and all that lives. Sought by the adoration and love of the soul, it reveals itself as the Godhead, we see in it the face of God and know the bliss of our Lover....

Brahman always reveals himself to us in three ways, within ourselves, above our plane, around us in the universe. Within us, there are two centres of the Purusha, the inner soul through which he touches us to our awakening; there is the Purusha in the lotus of the heart which opens upward all our powers and the Purusha in the thousand-petalled lotus whence descend through the thought and will, opening the third eye in us, the lightnings of vision and the fire of the divine energy. The bliss existence may come to us through either one of these centres. When the lotus of the heart breaks open, we feel a divine joy, love and peace expanding in us like a flower of light which irradiates the whole being.... When the other upper lotus opens, the whole mind becomes full of a divine light, joy and power, behind which is the Divine, the Lord of our being on his throne with our soul beside him or drawn inward into his rays; all the thoughts and will become then a luminosity, power and ecstasy.... The Divine reveals himself in the world around us when we look upon that with a spiritual desire of delight that seeks him in all things.... A universal spiritual Presence, a universal Peace, a universal infinite Delight has manifested, immanent, embracing, all-penetrating.... This is the Divine seen around us and on our own physical plane. But he may reveal himself above. We see or feel him as a high-uplifted Presence, a great infinite of Ananda above us—or in it, our Father in heaven—and do not feel or see him in ourselves or around us.... The complete redemption comes by the descent of the divine Power into the human mind and body and the remoulding of their inner life into the divine image—what the Vedic seers called the birth of the Son by the sacrifice. It is in fact by a continual sacrifice or offering, a sacrifice of adoration and aspiration, of works, of thought and knowledge, of the mounting flame of the godward will that we build ourselves into the being of this Infinite.

SRI AUROBINDO, The Synthesis of Yoga,
III, ch. VII.

70. Still, the more varied and most intimate experience of divine love cannot come by the pursuit of the impersonal Infinite alone.... The Divine is a Being and not an abstract existence or a status of pure timeless infinity; the original and universal existence is He, but that existence is inseparable from consciousness and bliss of being, and an existence conscious of its own being and its own bliss is what we may well call a divine infinite Person—Purusha. Moreover, all consciousness implies power, Shakti; where there is infinite consciousness of being, there is infinite power of being, and by that power all exists in the universe.... It is to this Godhead, this Being that the Bhakti of an integral Yoga will be poured out and uplifted. Transcendent, it will seek him in the ecstasy of an absolute union; universal, it will seek him in infinite quality and every aspect and in all beings with a universal delight and love; individual, it will enter into all human relations with him that love

creates between person and person.... He is the friend, the adviser, helper, saviour in trouble and distress, the defender from enemies, the hero who fights our battles for us or under whose shield we fight, the charioteer, the pilot of our ways. And here we come at once to a closer intimacy; he is the comrade and eternal companion, the playmate of the game of living. But still there is so far a certain division, however pleasant, and friendship is too much limited by the appearance of beneficence. The lover can wound, abandon, be wroth with us, seem to betray, yet our love endures and even grows by these oppositions; they increase the joy of reunion and the joy of possession; through them the lover remains the friend, and all that he does, we find in the end, has been done by the lover and helper of our being for our soul's perfection as well as for his joy in us.

These contradictions lead to a greater intimacy. He is the father and the mother too of our being, its source and protector and its indulgent cherisher and giver of our desires. He is the child born to our desire whom we cherish and rear. All these things the lover takes up; his love in its intimacy and oneness keeps in it the paternal and maternal care and lend itself to our demands upon it. All is unified in that deepest many-sided relation.... Love and Ananda are the last word of being, the secret of secrets, the mystery of mysteries.

SRI AUROBINDO, The Synthesis of Yoga,
III, ch. VIII.

71.   [The Divine Grace, we give it that name] because we feel in the infinite Spirit or Self or Existence a Presence or a Being, a Consciousness that determines—that is what we speak of as the Divine—not a separate person, but the one Being of whom our individual self is a portion or a vessel.... It is an action from above or from within independent of mental causes which decides its own movement. We can call it the Divine Grace; we can call it the Self within choosing its own hour and way to manifest to the mental instrument on the sur-

face; we can call it the flowering of the inner being or inner nature into self-realisation and self-knowledge. As something in us approaches it or as it presents itself to us, so the mind sees it. But in reality it is the same thing and the same process of the being in Nature.
SRI AUROBINDO, *On Yoga, II, tome I,*
part II, 3.

72. Krishna's Grace calls whom it wills to call without any determining reason for the choice or the rejection, it is all his mercy, or else he calls the hearts that are ready to vibrate and leap up at his call—and even there he waits till the moment has come.... It does not depend on outward merit or appearance of fitness.... The Gopis heard and rushed out into the forest —the others did not, or did they think it was only some rustic music or some rude cowherd-lover fluting to his sweetheart: not a call that learned and cultured or virtuous ears could recognise as the call of the Divine?... Some may have the *adhikāra* (readiness, preparation) for recognising Krishna's flute, some for the call of Christ, some for the dance of Shiva—to each his own way and his nature's answer to the Divine call.
SRI AUROBINDO, *On Yoga, II, tome I,*
part II, 7.

IV

LOVE AND ANANDA IN THE TRANSFORMED MANIFESTATION

73. The meeting of man and God must always mean a penetration and entry of the Divine into the human and a self-immergence of man in the Divinity.

But that immergence is not in the nature of an annihilation. Extinction is not the fulfilment of all this search and passion, suffering and rapture. The game would never have been begun if that were to be its ending.

SRI AUROBINDO, Thoughts and Glimpses.

74. What is there new that we have yet to accomplish? Love, for as yet we have only accomplished hatred and self-pleasing; Knowledge, for as yet we have only accomplished error and perception and conceiving; Bliss, for as yet we have only accomplished pleasure and pain and indifference; Power, for as yet we have only accomplished weakness and effort and a defeated victory; Life, for as yet we have only accomplished birth and growth and dying; Unity, for as yet we have only accomplished war and association.

In a word, godhead; to remake ourselves in the divine image.

Ibid.

75. If mankind only caught a glimpse of what infinite enjoyments, what perfect forces, what luminous reaches of spontaneous knowledge, what wide calms of our being lie waiting for us in the tracts which our animal evolution has not yet conquered, they would leave all and never rest till they had gained these treasures. But the way is narrow, the doors are hard to force, and fear, distrust and scepticism are there, tentacles of Nature to forbid the turning away of our feet from less ordinary pastures.

      SRI AUROBINDO, *Thoughts and Aphorisms*, 5.

76. THE HIDDEN PLAN

However long Night's hour, I will not dream
  That the small ego and the person's mask
Are all that God reveals in our life-scheme,
  The last result of Nature's cosmic task.
A greater Presence in her bosom works;
  Long it prepares its far epiphany:
Even in the stone and beast the godhead lurks,
  A bright Persona of eternity.
It shall burst out from the limit traced by Mind
  And make a witness of the prescient heart;
It shall reveal even in this inert blind
  Nature, long veiled in each inconscient part,
Fulfilling the occult magnificent plan,
The world-wide and immortal spirit in man.

      SRI AUROBINDO, *Last Poems*.

77.

A Voice ill-heard shall speak, the soul obey,
A power into mind's inner chamber steal,
A charm and sweetness open life's closed doors
And beauty conquer the resisting world,
The truth-light capture Nature by surprise,
A stealth of God compel the heart to bliss
And earth grow unexpectedly divine.
In Matter shall be lit the spirit's glow,
In body and body kindled the sacred birth;
Night shall awake to the anthem of the stars,
The days become a happy pilgrim march,
Our will a force of the Eternal's power,
And thought the rays of a spiritual sun.

A few shall see what none yet understands;
God shall grow up while the wise men talk and sleep;
For man shall not know the coming till its hour
And belief shall be not till the work is done.
                SRI AUROBINDO, *Savitri, Book I, Canto IV.*

78. The old spirituality was an escape from life towards the divine Reality, leaving the world where it was, as it was. Our new vision, on the contrary, is the divinisation of life, the transformation of the material into a divine world.... This work could have been a simple continuation, an amelioration, an enlargement of the old world as it was.... But what has happened is truly a new thing, a new world has been born. It is not the old that is being transformed, it is quite a new world that has been really concretely born.

At the present hour we are in the very heart of a period of transition, where the two are intertwined: the old persists, still all powerful, and continues to dominate the ordinary consciousness, while the new glides in, still very modest, unnoticed to the extent that for the moment it disturbs nothing much externally....

In any case, to simplify one can say that the old world, the creation of what Sri Aurobindo calls the Overmind, was in a characteristic way the age of the gods and therefore the age of religions.... In the supramental creation there will no more be religions. All life will be the expression, the flowering in forms of the Divine Unity manifesting in the world. And there will be no more what men now call the gods.

These great divine beings themselves will be able to participate in the new creation, but for that they must put on what we may call the supramental substance on earth. And if there are some who choose to remain in their world, as they are, if they decide not to manifest themselves physically, their relation with the other beings of the supramental world on earth will be a relation of friends, of collaborators, of equal to equal, because the highest divine essence will have manifested in the beings of the new supramental world on earth.

When the physical substance will be supramentalised, to be born on earth in a body will not be a cause of inferiority; rather the contrary, there will be gained a plenitude which could not be obtained otherwise....

I invite you to the great adventure, and in this adventure you are not to repeat spiritually what others have done before us, because our adventure begins from beyond that stage. We are for a new creation, entirely new, carrying in it all the unforeseen, all risks, all hazards,—a true adventure of which the goal is sure victory, but of which the way is unknown and has to be traced out step by step in the unexplored.

THE MOTHER, Questions and Answers,
Bulletin, Nov. 1957.

79. The gnosis is the effective principle of the Spirit, a highest dynamis of the spiritual existence. The gnostic individual would be the consummation of the spiritual man; his whole way of being, thinking, living, acting would be governed by the power of a vast universal spirituality.... He would feel the presence of the Divine in every centre of his consciousness, in every vibration of his life-force, in every cell of his body. In all the workings of his force of Nature he would be aware of the workings of the supreme World-Mother, the Supernature; he would see his natural being as the becoming and the manifestation of the power of the World-Mother. In this consciousness he would live and act in an entire transcendent freedom, a complete joy of the spirit, an entire identity with the cosmic self and a spontaneous sympathy with all in the universe. All beings would be to him his own selves, all ways and powers of consciousness would be felt as the ways and powers of his own universality.... His own life and the world life would be to him like a perfect work of art; it would be as if the creation of a cosmic and spontaneous genius infallible in its working out of a multitudinous order. The gnostic individual would be in the world and of the world, but would also exceed it in his consciousness and live in his self of transcendence above it; he would be universal but free in the universe, individual but not limited by a separative individuality....

One in self with all, the supramental being will seek the delight of self-manifestation of the Spirit in himself but equally the delight of the Divine in all: he will have the cosmic joy and will be a power for bringing the bliss of the spirit, the joy of being to others; for their joy will be part of his own joy of existence.... His feeling of universality, his action of universality will be always a spontaneous state and natural movement, an automatic expression of the Truth, an act of the joy of the spirit's self-existence. There could be in it no place for limited self or desire or for the satisfaction or frustration of the limited self or the satisfaction or frustration of desire, no place for the relative and dependent happiness and grief that visit and afflict our limited nature; for these are things that belong to the ego and the Ignorance, not to the freedom and truth of the Spirit.... The gnostic existence and delight of existence is a universal and total being and delight, and there will be the presence of that totality and universality in each separate movement: in each there will be, not a partial experience of self or a fractional bit of his joy, but the sense of the whole movement of an integral being and the presence of its entire and integral bliss of being, Ananda.

The gnostic life will be an inner life in which the antinomy of the inner and the outer, the self and the world will have been cured and exceeded. The gnostic being will have indeed an inmost existence in which he is alone with God, one with the Eternal, self-plunged into the depths of the Infinite, in communion with its heights and its luminous abysses of secrecy; nothing will be able to disturb or to invade these depths or bring him down from the summits, neither the world's contents not his action nor all that is around him. This is the transcendence aspect of the spiritual life and it is necessary for the freedom of the spirit; for otherwise the identity in Nature with the world would be a binding limitation and not a free identity. But at the same time God-love and the delight of God will be the heart's expression of that inner communion and oneness, and that delight and love will expand itself to embrace all existence. The peace of God within will be extended in the gnostic experience of the universe into a universal calm of equality not merely passive but dynamic, a calm of freedom in oneness dominating all that meets it, tranquillising all that enters into it, imposing its law of peace on the supramental being's relations with the world in which he is living.... It is this poise and freedom in the spirit that will enable him to take all life into himself while still remaining the spiritual self and to embrace even the world of the Ignorance without himself entering into the Ignorance....

Love will be for him the contact, meeting, union of self with self, of spirit with spirit, a unification of being, a power and joy and intimacy and closeness of soul to soul, of the One to the One, a joy of identity and the consequences of a diverse identity. It is the joy of an intimate self-revealing diversity of the One, the multitudinous union of the One and a happy interaction in the identity, that will be for him the full revealed sense of life. Creation aesthetic or dynamic, mental creation, life creation, material creation will have for him the same sense. It will be the creation of significant forms of the Eternal Force, Light, Beauty, Reality,—the beauty and truth of its forms and bodies, the beauty and truth of its powers and qualities, the beauty and truth of its spirit, its formless beauty of self and essence.

As a consequence of the total change and reversal of consciousness establishing a new relation of spirit with mind and life and matter, and a new significance and perfection in the relation, there will be a reversal, a perfecting new significance also of the relations between the spirit and the body it inhabits.

Peace and ecstasy cease to be different and become one.... This calm and this delight rise together, as one state, into an increasing intensity and culminate in the eternal ecstasy, the bliss that is the Infinite... this fundamental ecstasy of being...

translates [in the mind] into a calm of intense delight of spiritual perception and vision and knowledge, in the heart into a wide or deep or passionate delight of universal union and love and sympathy and the joy of beings and the joy of things. In the will and vital parts it is felt as the energy of delight of a divine life-power in action or a beatitude of the senses perceiving and meeting the One everywhere, perceiving as their normal aesthesis of things a universal beauty and a secret harmony of creation of which our mind can catch only imperfect glimpses or a rare supernormal sense. In the body it reveals itself as an ecstasy pouring into it from the heights of the spirit and the peace and bliss of a pure and spiritualised physical existence. A universal beauty and glory of being begins to manifest; all objects reveal hidden lines, vibrations, powers, harmonic significances concealed from the normal mind and the physical sense. In the universal phenomenon is revealed the eternal Ananda.

SRI AUROBINDO, *The Life Divine*, ch. 55,
or *The Future Evolution of Man*, VIII.

80. A spiritual or gnostic being would feel his harmony with the whole gnostic life around him, whatever his position in the whole. According to his place in it he would know how to lead or to rule, but also how to subordinate himself; both would be to him an equal delight: for the spirit's freedom, because it is eternal, self-existent and inalienable, can be felt as much in service and willing subordination and adjustment with other selves as in power and rule. An inner spiritual freedom can accept its place in the truth of an inner spiritual hierarchy as well as in the truth, not incompatible with it, of a fundamental spiritual equality. It is this self-arrangement of Truth, a natural order of the spirit, that would exist in a common life of different degrees and stages of the evolving gnostic being. Unity is the basis of the gnostic consciousness, mutuality the natural result of its direct awareness of oneness in diversity, harmony the inevitable power of the working of its force. Unity, mutuality and harmony must therefore be the inescapable law of a common or collective gnostic life. What forms it might take would depend upon the will of evolutionary manifestation of the Supernature, but this would be its general character and principle....

The one rule of the gnostic life would be the self-expression of the Spirit, the will of the Divine Being; that will, that self-expression could manifest through extreme simplicity or through extreme complexity and opulence or in their natural balance, —for beauty and plenitude, a hidden sweetness and laughter in things, a sunshine and gladness of life are also powers and expressions of the Spirit. In all directions the Spirit within determining the law of the nature would determine the frame of the life and its detail and circumstance. In all there would be the same plastic principle; a rigid standardization, however necessary for the mind's arrangement of things, could not be the law of the spiritual life. A great diversity and liberty of self-expression based on an underlying unity might well become manifest; but everywhere there would be harmony and truth of order.

A life of gnostic beings carrying the evolution to a higher supramental status might fitly be characterized as a divine life; for it would be a life in the Divine, a life of the beginnings of a spiritual divine light and power and joy manifested in material Nature. That might be described, since it surpasses the mental human level, as a life of spiritual and supramental supermanhood. But this must not be confused with past and present ideas of supermanhood; for supermanhood in the mental idea consists of an overtopping of the normal human level, not in kind but in degree of the same kind, by an enlarged personality, a magnified and exaggerated ego, an increased power of mind, an increased power of vital force, a refined or dense and massive exaggeration of the forces of the human Ignorance; it carries also, commonly implied in it, the idea of a forceful domination over humanity by the superman. That would mean a supermanhood of the Nietzschean type; it might be at its worst the reign of the 'blond beast' or the dark beast or of any and every beast, a return to barbaric strength and ruthlessness and force: but this would be no evolution, it would be a reversion to an old strenuous barbarism.

But earth has had enough of this kind in her past and its repetition can only prolong the old lines; she can get no true profit for her future, no power of self-exceeding, from the Titan, the Asura: even a great or supernormal power in it could only carry her on larger circles of her old orbit. But what has to emerge is something much more difficult and much more simple; it is a self-realized being, a building of the spiritual self, an intensity and urge of the soul and the deliverance and sovereignty of its light and power and beauty,—not an egoistic supermanhood seizing on a mental and vital domination over humanity, but the sovereignty of the Spirit over its own instruments, its possession of itself and its possession of life in the power of the spirit, a new consciousness in which humanity itself shall find its own self-exceeding and self-fulfilment by the revelation of the divinity that is striving for birth within it. This is the sole true supermanhood and the one real possibility of a step forward in evolutionary Nature.

SRI AUROBINDO, *The Life Divine*, ch. 56,
or *The Future Evolution of Man*, IX.

81.   "O Satyavan, O luminous Savitri,
I sent you forth of old beneath the stars,
A dual power of God in an ignorant world,
In a hedged creation shut from limitless self,
Bringing down God to the insentient glow,
Lifting earth-beings to immortality.
....

"He is my soul that climbs from nescient Night
Through life and mind and Supernature's Vast
To the supernal light of Timelessness
And my eternity hid in moving Time
And my boundlessness cut by the curve of Space.
....

"O Savitri, thou art my spirit's Power,
The revealing voice of my immortal Word,
The face of Truth upon the roads of Time
Pointing to the souls of men the routes to God.
....

"Abandoning the dubious Middle Way
A few shall glimpse the miraculous Origin
And some shall feel in you the secret Force
And they shall turn to meet a nameless tread,
Adventurers into a mightier Day.
Ascending out of the limiting breadths of mind,
They shall discover the world's huge design
And step into the Truth, the Right, the Vast.
You shall reveal to them the hidden eternities,
The breath of infinitudes not yet revealed,
Some rapture of the bliss that made the world,
Some rush of the force of God's omnipotence,
Some beam of the omniscient Mystery.
But when the hour of the Divine draws near,
The Mighty Mother shall take birth in Time
And God be born into the human clay
In forms made ready by your human lives.
Then shall the Truth supreme be given to men.
....

"The incarnate dual Power shall open God's door,
Eternal supermind touch earthly Time.
The superman shall wake in mortal man
And manifest the hidden demi-god
Or grow into the God-Light and God-Force
Revealing the secret deity in the cave.
....

"A mightier race shall inhabit the mortal's world.
On Nature's luminous tops, on the Spirit's ground,
The superman shall reign as king of life,
Make earth almost the mate and peer of heaven

And lead towards God and truth man's ignorant heart
And lift towards godhead his mortality.
....

"A divine harmony shall be earth's law,
Beauty and Joy remould her way to live :
....

"Even should a hostile force cling to its reign
And claim its right's perpetual sovereignty
And man refuse his high spiritual fate,
Yet shall the secret Truth in things prevail.
For in the march of all-fulfilling Time
The hour must come of the Transcendent's will :
All turns and winds towards his predestined ends
In Nature's fixed inevitable course
Decreed since the beginning of the worlds
In the deep essence of created things :
....

"Even the many shall some answer make
And bear the splendour of the Divine's rush
And his impetuous knock at unseen doors.
A heavenlier passion shall upheave men's lives,
Their mind shall share in the ineffable gleam,
Their heart shall feel the ecstasy and the fire,
Earth's bodies shall be conscious of a soul;
Mortality's bond-slaves shall unloose their bonds,
Mere men into spiritual beings grow
And see awake the dumb divinity.
....

"Thus shall the earth open to divinity
And common natures feel the wide uplift,
Illumine common acts with the Spirit's ray
And meet the deity in common things.
Nature shall live to manifest secret God,
The Spirit shall take up the human play,
This earthly life become the life divine."
....

The prophet moment covered limitless space'
And cast into the heart of hurrying Time
A diamond light of the Eternal's peace,
A crimson seed of God's felicity;
A glance from the gaze fell of undying Love.
....
A power leaned down, a happiness found its home.
Over wide earth brooded the infinite bliss.

SRI AUROBINDO, *Savitri*, Bk. XI,
The Book of Everlasting Day.

GLOSSARY OF SANSKRIT TERMS

adhikāra : fitness, capacity for attaining to the Divine
ānanda : essential Delight, spiritual Bliss
asura : a being (usually) of the invisible mentalised vital world, whose characteristic is an effective intelligence put at the service of spiritual Darkness and ignorant egoism, and therefore hostile to the Divine and the divine Light
ātman : Self or Spirit; has two aspects, universal and individual
avatāra : avatar—a divine incarnation, fully conscious; the number of avatars varies (the ancient Scriptures have named 32); the major avatars are:
  1 *matsya*—fish
  2 *kūrma*—tortoise
  3 *varāha*—boar
  4 *narasiṃha*—man-lion
  5 *vāmana*—dwarf
  6 *paraśu-rāma*—incarnation of the Power aspect of the Divine
  7 *rāma (rāma-candra)*—Rama (Rama-Chandra)
      —fights and conquers the *asura* (s)
  8 *kṛṣṇa*—Krishna
  9 *buddha*—the Buddha
 10 *kalki*—Kalki
bhakta : lover and devotee of the Divine
bhakti : devotion to the Divine
brahman : the absolute, omnipresent Reality; the eternal Spirit, Origin and Self of the universe
Chaitanya : Bengali religious reformer and creator of a powerful *bhakti* movement (1485–1527); often listed among the avatars as he was frequently though momentarily possessed by the Divine, and the possession was full while it lasted

dharma : law, norm, rule of being, life and action
gopī : girl(s) playmate(s) of child Krishna when keeping the cows
jīvātman : the individual Self or Spirit
kalki : Kalki—the last avatar, symbolically described as riding a white horse
kṛṣṇa : Krishna—one of the major avatars, the most famous hero of the epic Scriptures of India and her most popular Divinity
līlā : the cosmic play or game; the world regarded as a play of the Divine
nirguṇa : "without qualities", i.e. above the qualities or modes of Nature
ojas : the spiritual energy in man
parameśvara : the Divine as Lord of Nature and Master of the universe
prakṛti : Prakriti, Nature, in opposition to the Soul or conscious Being *(puruṣa)*
pralaya : cosmic dissolution, return of the universe to the unmanifested state
puruṣha : Purusha, the Soul or conscious Being whose presence supports the operations of Nature *(prakṛti)* and gives them a direction by assent or dissent
puruṣottama : Purushottama, the supreme Personality, the Supreme
retas : in man, the subtle energy turned towards procreation
saccidānanda : sat-cit-ānanda, Sachchidananda, Sat-Chit-Ananda, transcendent Existence, Self-Awareness and Delight, the highest description of the supreme Reality
sādhaka : one who practises a spiritual discipline
sādhanā : spiritual discipline and practice
śakti : Shakti, the creative conscious Power of the Divine as Lord of the universe
vibhūti : a minor and partial incarnation of the Divine, i.e. a manifestation upon earth of a divine Power (strength, beauty, glory, knowledge, love...) only partially conscious

of its divine origin, while the avatar is a complete and fully conscious manifestation of the Supreme

viśvakāma : universal lust, i.e. sexual desire for all

viśvaprema : universal love, i.e. love for all

yoga : 1) union with the Self, the Spirit or the Divine
2) a spiritual practice and discipline that makes this union possible

yogī : one who practises a discipline leading to the union with the Self, the Spirit or the Divine